VENTURE OUT!

An Entrepreneurial Introduction to Business

Third Edition

Monty L. Lynn
Abilene Christian University

Cover design by Doris Bruey
Book design by Monty L. Lynn

Copyright 2008 by Monty L. Lynn

All rights reserved. No part of this book may be reproduced or utilized in any form or by any means, electronic or mechanical, including photocopying and recording, or by any informational storage and retrieval system without written permission from the publisher.

Books may be purchased for educational purposes.

For information, please call or write:

   1-800-586-0330

   Fountainhead Press
   2140 E. Southlake Blvd., Suite L, #816
   Southlake, TX 76092

Web site: www.fountainheadpress.com
Email: customerservice@fountainheadpress.com

Third Edition

ISBN: 978-1-59871-123-3

Printed in the United States of America

TABLE OF CONTENTS

- 1   INTRODUCTION
- 5   TASK 1: TEAMBUILDING
- 11   TASK 2: PLANNING
- 19   TASK 3: ORGANIZING
- 20   TASK 4: EXPLORING
- 20   TASK 5: RESEARCHING
- 20   TASK 6: PROPOSING
- 20   TASK 7: FUNDING AND ORDERING
- 20   TASK 8: SELLING
- 20   TASK 9: REPORTING
- 20   TASK 10: CELEBRATING
- 20   APPENDIX A: FREQUENTLY ASKED QUESTIONS

INTRODUCTION

The Venture Out project is an engaging and fun way to introduce basic business concepts. It brings various functions of business together in a simulated business so you can experience what life is like in a small start-up company.

You'll form a team, research a market, select a product, write a business plan, and present your plan to a board of judges. If your team loan is approved, you'll order and sell your product. Your profits will be used for a worthy beneficiary. Throughout Venture Out, you'll learn about effective teamwork which is essential in business. At the conclusion of the project, your team will produce a professional annual report summarizing your company's performance and lessons learned. From start-up to harvest, management to product design, accounting to sales—you'll experience it all.

Venture Out emphasizes:

- Active learning - *You'll put business concepts and theory into action*
- Integration - *You'll see how various sub-disciplines in business work together*
- Teamwork - *You'll experience the challenges and rewards of working with others*
- Service - *You'll offer value to your customers and a beneficiary*
- Leadership and project management - *You'll plan and execute a project*

GOALS

There are innumerable opportunities to be creative and to grow—look for them along the way and keep in mind three overarching goals:

- Goal #1: Learn

    Individually and as a team, reflect on what you are experiencing and learning in Venture Out. What does it take to be successful in various parts of the venture? What are your gifts, interests, and skills? What are you learning in working with others and in the details of accounting, marketing, and working with suppliers? How can you grow in your effectiveness?

- Goal #2: Be ethical and professional and continue to give back to society

    In everything you do, and with every person you work with—lenders, customers, suppliers, other students and beneficiaries—treat others with respect and professionalism. Demonstrate social responsibility in product choice and remember that your actions won't be confined to a term paper or exam. They will be public and you will be working with small and large businesses. Your actions reflect on yourself, your team, your major, your instructor, and your institution. Commerce is built on a foundation of trust and the stewardship of limited and shared resources. Be responsible and ethical as you act.

- Goal #3: Make a profit

    If businesses don't generate a profit, there are no revenues, jobs, or services to share with others. Even not-for-profit organizations generally attempt to make a profit—they reinvest those profits in their organization for future growth rather than passing them along to owners. You may discover that the discipline of competitive markets—the pressure to be profitable—can sharpen your ability to see business opportunities, deliver value to customers, find solutions to problems, and earn a profit.

Many individuals involved in Venture Out want you to succeed, but ultimately, you and your team are responsible for a successful venture.

A TRAIL GUIDE

This manual is like a trail guide: It recommends a path but it can't predict every fork in the road, hazard, or exciting vista along the way. We've removed some of the obstacles but since you're dealing with real life events, lots of choices remain. These can be some of the best learning environments, where the directions point the way but there's room to choose, create, and act. Be vigilant and watchful because you can bet that some parts of the trail will be steep, sudden squalls can develop, and there's much to learn along the way. That's part of the thrill of business.

Tasks are laid out each week to simulate the path a new business venture might follow. Some weeks, you'll have more to do than other weeks. Occasionally, your team may need to meet outside of class. If you complete all of a week's tasks, you may want to look ahead toward the coming task, but don't work ahead more than one week without the approval of your instructor.

Be sure to read and follow each week's instructions carefully. In addition to these, your instructor may provide Venture Out guidelines that are specific to your campus. We'll remind you each week to check these.

To assist you in identifying tasks to be completed, tasks are labeled with the following abbreviations:

- FINA = Finance and Accounting Group

    This group prepares all the financial statements and manages revenue and expenses

- MARP = Marketing and Production Group

   This group manages all aspects of the product, marketing, and sales

- MGMT = Management Group

   This group facilitates effective teamwork, records important information, and assembles the business plan and the annual report

- TEAM = All team members

   Some items need everyone's participation; when you see the TEAM designation, it means the entire team works together on a task, or in the case of homework, all members work alone

Be sure to bring this manual to each Venture Out meeting so you will know the tasks to complete that day or week.

ACKNOWLEDGMENTS

The Venture Out approach to introducing business has been utilized at several colleges and universities over the years. Two individuals inspired many of these applications:

- Dr. John Miller, a management professor at Bucknell University, employed a hands-on, team-based approach in management education over thirty years ago and then graciously shared his ideas and experiences with colleagues around the world.

- Dr. Larry Michaelsen, a management professor at Central Missouri State University, has helped many professors and students engage large classes in innovative ways.

Many at Abilene Christian University have supported Venture Out too including dean Rick Lytle, students Jennifer Swenson, Beth Wright, Colby Blackwell, and Savannah Slagel, several loan review judges, and a few bankers, including most recently, Krista Fauvel.

This Venture Out guidebook has been developed and tested by hundreds of Abilene Christian University students who consistently impress me with their persistence, creativity, and promise. It is to them—students in the Introduction to Business and Technology course—that this manual is dedicated.

I welcome your suggestions for improving this manual or the Venture Out program.

Dr. Monty L. Lynn, WW Caruth Chair of Management
College of Business Administration
Abilene Christian University
Abilene, Texas 79699
monty.lynn@coba.acu.edu

TASK 1: TEAMBUILDING

"Our task is not to see through one another but to see one another through."

~ Paul R. Van Gorder

OVERVIEW

- Divide into companies (TEAM)
- Nurture *esprit-de-corps* by getting to know your team members (TEAM)
- Divide your team into groups (TEAM)
- Homework: Set up a record keeping system (MGMT)
- Homework: Familiarize yourself with the steps ahead in Venture Out (TEAM)

DETAILS

1. Divide into companies (TEAM)

   Your instructor will divide you into teams and assign you a temporary team name. This will be your company for the remainder of Venture Out.

2. Review today's tasks and any special instructions from your instructor (TEAM)

   Look over today's tasks and decide as a group how much time to devote to each task. Then choose someone to serve as today's timekeeper to help you stay on schedule—perhaps the person whose birthday is closest to today. Then work through the tasks listed for today.

3. Nurture *esprit-de-corps* by getting to know your team members (TEAM)

   Relax and take some time to get to know your teammates. Try to remember each person's name and establish an informal and friendly climate where everyone feels comfortable to contribute. To help with introductions, try the three exercises below:

   Getting Started – Introduce yourself by responding to these easy questions:

   - What is your name?
   - What is your major? What do you want to do with it?

- What do you consider to be your hometown? Describe where it is if others don't know.

In My Wildest Dreams[1] – Whether big and outrageous, or simple and immediate—like getting through this week—invite each team member to finish these sentences:

- I'd spend more time…
- I'd visit…
- I'd learn…
- I'd drive…
- I'd have lunch with…

Best Team[2] – As a final exercise, take a few moments to recall a team that you were part of that was fun and successful. Silently answer these questions (jot notes if you wish):

- Why was this group best?
- What made this team special?
- What really stands out in your mind about this team?

Together, consolidate your memories and make a list of key success factors for successful teamwork. Try to breakdown broad items like "communication" and "leadership." *The team member who was born closest to January 1 should be the note taker for this exercise. Your instructor may request that these notes be added to your team notebook or discussed in class.*

4. Divide your team into groups (TEAM)

The next step is for every member of the company to join one of three groups. The three groups function like departments within a company:

- Finance and Accounting (FINA)
- Marketing and Production (MARP)

---

[1] Questions were selected from Toben and Joanne Heim, *What's Your Story?* (Colorado Springs, CO: Piñon, 1999).

[2] Adapted from Dennis O'Connor and Leodones Yballe, "Team Leadership: Critical Steps to Great Projects," *Journal of Management Education*, April 2007, 292-312.

- Management (MGMT)

Read the job descriptions for each team and devise a method for forming groups so everyone is satisfied with their assignment. Each team should be subdivided into three groups of approximately equal size. As Venture Out progresses, each group can decide how to allocate jobs to different group and team members. You'll learn something important about business regardless of the group you are in, so don't worry if you don't get in the group related to your major or professional interests.

In newly formed teams, some members may be hesitant to state their opinions. Take care to insure that everyone feels comfortable speaking openly about preferences and is happy with the group they join.

Since Venture Out teams operate without a hierarchy (you could choose a president if you wish but one is not specified in this manual), everyone needs to lead in their area. Although you may work most often with one group, your team will function best when everyone knows what the others are doing and helps the team succeed. You can do this by instituting two regular practices:

- Keep the team informed of your group's progress (needs, challenges, etc.)

- Provide appropriate accountability and support for team members—if someone is not pulling their weight, try to get them involved; if someone is struggling, try to help them

The most understated challenge and reward in Venture Out is teamwork. Nothing is more challenging or rewarding than communicating clearly and honestly, being dependable and professional, and relying on each other for expertise. We'll share suggestions on how to hone your teamwork skills throughout this manual, but much will rely on your actions as individual team members and the culture you establish together.

THE TEAM'S JOB DESCRIPTION

Every team member should perform these essential skills and job functions:

- Actively participate, contribute ideas, and do your share of the work
- Listen to others and communicate assertively and respectfully
- Hold one another accountable
- Produce high-quality work on time
- Strive for high performance in all aspects of your work
- Sell your portion of the product and help keep your team on schedule
- Contribute to the business plan and annual report

FINANCE AND ACCOUNTING GROUP (FINA)

Be detail-oriented, responsible with money, spreadsheet proficient, and :

- Prepare financial statements for the loan application and annual report
- Prepare a budget scenario worksheet
- Keep precise records of all financial transactions
- Audit budget variance and insure groups stay within their budgets
- Be responsible for collecting and depositing cash
- Obtain reimbursements for expenses

MARKETING AND PRODUCTION GROUP (MARP)

Interact effectively with suppliers and customers, think creatively, problem-solve, and:

- Generate and research product ideas, possible suppliers, and product pricing
- Order and manage product inventory
- Recommend promotional strategy
- Arrange for sales locations on campus and any promotional materials
- Track and manage sales performance

MANAGEMENT GROUP (MGMT)

Write and edit well, be proficient in word processing, effectively motivate individual team members, facilitate the work of a cross-functional team, and:

- Prepare a team member directory
- Set up a collection point for team materials—a notebook or electronic tool
- Motivate others to do their best
- Assemble, edit, produce, and present a professional business plan and final report

5. Homework: Set up a record keeping system (a MGMT group member with organizational and perhaps technology skills should do this before your next meeting)

   Start organizing a place to collect Venture Out materials and records. This could be a notebook which is brought to each team meeting or an electronic document sharing tool like Microsoft Groove or Google Docs. Choose a system that's organized, secure, and accessible to your Venture Out team during meetings. The documents you gather will be used to build your business plan and annual report. Be sure to label your physical folder (if applicable) with your name and contact information or have a backup of files if you keep your documents electronically. You won't want to lose these important documents.

6. Homework: Familiarize yourself with the steps ahead in Venture Out (TEAM)

   - Browse the Introduction and Appendix A
   - Respond to the questions in "Are You a Team Player"

ARE YOU A TEAM PLAYER?

Team effectiveness requires knowing yourself as well as how teams work. Recall a time when you experienced success in a team. Then respond to the questions below and see if you can identify strengths you can exercise in your team and developmental areas you might stretch. For each row, check the space in the column that best describes your behavior.

	Often like me	Sometimes like me	Sometimes like me	Often like me	
I consider points of view besides my own	___	___	___	___	I resist new or different points of view
I'm a perfectionist	___	___	___	___	Little mistakes don't bother me
I talk a lot in group discussions	___	___	___	___	I don't talk much when in a group
I'm a good listener	___	___	___	___	I tune others out
I express my opinions without any intimidation	___	___	___	___	When I express my opinions, I do it carefully
I don't flinch when I have to confront someone	___	___	___	___	Avoidance is how I deal with conflict
I like being in charge and leading others	___	___	___	___	I prefer that others be in charge and lead
I go out of my way to help others	___	___	___	___	I prefer to stick to my own tasks
I like to take risks	___	___	___	___	I prefer safety
I get impatient when a group gets off task	___	___	___	___	It doesn't both me when a group wanders
I'm highly organized	___	___	___	___	I'm disorganized
Groups are motivated and fun when I'm a member	___	___	___	___	I don't affect team motivation and fun
I can think up creative solutions	___	___	___	___	I think of standard solutions
I open the door for others to participate	___	___	___	___	I leave quiet members to themselves
I can consider criticism without it bothering me	___	___	___	___	My feelings get hurt easily
I pour my energy into group projects	___	___	___	___	I overly depend on others in group projects
I like to have everything planned	___	___	___	___	I like to act spontaneously
I finish work ahead of time	___	___	___	___	I start things close to the deadline

TASK 2: PLANNING

"Good results without good planning come from good luck not good management."

~ David Jaquith

OVERVIEW

- Refresh yourselves on names and welcome any new team members (TEAM)
- Take minutes (MGMT)
- Prepare a company directory (MGMT)
- Write a company mission statement (TEAM)
- Set company rules and boundaries (TEAM)
- Homework: Watch for campus opportunities (TEAM)

DETAILS

1. Refresh yourselves on names and welcome any new team members (TEAM)

    Be sure everyone knows everyone else's name on your team, and everyone is in a group they are excited about. If any students have joined late, welcome them and affiliate them with a group.

2. Take minutes (MGMT)

    Ask someone to take minutes today of your meeting and be sure to add the minutes to the notebook set up in the homework from Task 1. You'll decide later who will take minutes at each of your other meetings. There may not be much to record today, but it's a good habit to begin practicing.

    It is especially important to make note of attendance, decisions, actions, and assignments, such as: "Ravi will check on suppliers for our product idea and report back next week," or "Becca will get permission for us to sell at the football games," etc. Minutes clarify communication, jog your memory, and facilitate accountability. Here's an example:

> ### TEAM BLUE MINUTES
>
> September 12—10:00-10:45 a.m.
> Absent: Jessica
> Minutes taken by: Luke
>
> - Met members of team who were not at first meeting
> - Gathered information (names, email, phone) from each member for the team directory; MGMT will email the list to all members and the instructor (in notebook)
> - Richard volunteered to take minutes today
> - Roles were outlined for groups and individuals; all agreed to roles and responsibilities (in notebook)
> - Team members set company rules and boundaries (in notebook)
> - Drafted a mission statement (in notebook)
> - Briefly brainstormed product ideas—baseball cap, tee-shirt, lawn chair
> - Homework: All report back at the next meeting with at least one product idea

3. Prepare a company directory (MGMT)

   A MGMT team member should:

   - Compile an employee directory: Collect first and last names, e-mail addresses, phone numbers, groups they are a member of (FINA, MARP, or MGMT) of all team members.

   - E-mail your list: E-mail a copy of your list to your instructor, student coach(es) (if applicable), and your teammates—do this today! Be sure to include your team's temporary name (e.g., Team Wildcat) and your course section. Some teams might wish to set up other communication aids such as a Facebook or email group or include contact information on your Microsoft Groove or Google Docs site.

4. Write a company mission statement (TEAM)

   To stay on track, an organization needs to know its mission. Brief mission statements can be challenging to write because they require distilling the essence of an organization's purpose and values. Because Venture Out teams are small and short-term, writing a mission won't be too difficult. It is critical that everyone have a voice in the process. The "Tips for Writing a Mission Statement" at the end of this section provide some helpful guidelines.

5. Set company rules and boundaries (TEAM)

   As mentioned already, the most rewarding—and challenging—part of Venture Out is developing relationships that allow you to work effectively as a team. Part of this is just getting to know each other—learning which skills are present and absent from your team and how you can leverage your strengths and grow in weaker areas.

   At the beginning of a team's formation is the best time to set mutual expectations and rules for effective teamwork. If you wait until a problem develops and you've not discussed expectations, challenges become more difficult to handle. To help you get started on the right foot, draft some team principles, procedures, and roles.

   Principles

   Take a few minutes to consider carefully what you expect of each other and write these as "Accountability Principles." Someone from the MGMT group should record these principles and file them for later reference. If you write them and forget about them, they'll do you no good. But if you live by the principles you mutually accept, they will help you succeed together. Here's what to do:

   - Make a list of 4-6 behaviors you expect from each other. Consider attendance at meetings, timeliness and professionalism in completing tasks, keeping each other informed of progress and missing meetings, cooperative spirit and respect, etc.

   - Decide what you will do if someone doesn't meet the principles you agree upon. For example, what if someone misses a meeting and you don't hear from them, or a deadline is missed on a task. You don't have to decide on detailed actions or be punishing, but decide who will manage the situation and how.

   Procedures

   In addition to team principles, take some time to develop a team meeting routine. These will keep your team meetings orderly and productive. Although this is tedious work, it will increase your meeting productivity. Take a few moments to decide:

   - Who will lead company meetings? For example, will you rotate roles or let that naturally develop over time? (These roles are detailed below.) One advantage of rotating these roles among team members is that it gives everyone a chance to sharpen different group skills.

   - What will be your standard meeting format? You might begin with something like the following and adjust it as needed over time

     - Old business—Review any work in progress or tasks due today noted in last week's minutes

- New business—Review today's tasks and allocate an approximate amount of time to each
- Sum up—Conclude the meeting by reviewing who will do what, when, and where

Roles

Although you might create others, the basic roles to consider are:

- Discussion leader—This person initiates the discussion and keeps the team on task
- Minute taker—This person writes down the essence of the meeting's discussion, decisions, and tasks to do's, and gives them to the annual report assembler at the end of the meeting
- Timekeeper—This person makes sure the team is keeping the discussion moving well enough to complete the day's tasks

Good teams usually have members who play several unofficial roles too, such as those listed below. If you see a need in your team—for humor or someone to synthesize ideas or encourage quiet team members to share their ideas—help your company by playing that role! Being an effective team member means watching for opportunities to encourage others, notice problems, and smooth the group process so everyone is involved.

INFORMAL TEAM ROLES

Well-functioning teams often have members who play a variety of informal roles, including:

Task Roles

- Get the discussion started
- Call for action
- Seek information from others
- Offer opinions or provide information
- Get the team back on the task
- Evaluate ideas
- Summarize a discussion

Support Roles

- Encourage others
- Harmonize differing opinions
- Generate energy and enthusiasm
- Inject humor
- Facilitate compromise
- Involve quiet members
- Encourage accountability

Team Troubleshooting

In high-performance teams, team members complement each other and are committed to succeeding. It's common, however, even in high-performance teams, for problems to arise. Some common problems are presented in the Team Troubleshooting table below along with possible corrective actions. In many cases, it helps to communicate assertively and tactfully with one another about problems as they arise.

6. Homework: Watch for campus opportunities (TEAM)

    Don't worry yet about choosing a product. Simply notice possible opportunities that would be in demand on campus. Ask yourself: "What product need or desire is currently not being met on campus?"

    You can find ideas in catalogs, on the Internet, from other school experiences, from home, or elsewhere. But keep in mind that you need more than a "cool product" or a product "so cheap everyone can afford to buy one." According to entrepreneurship writer Jeffrey Timmons, a good business opportunity has three essential parts:

    An Opportunity = Idea + Demand + Profit

    You need a quality product that is competitively priced and distributed effectively (idea); consumers have to want it (demand), and; you have to be able to make money selling it (profit). A lot of novel inventions are not in demand and some things people would like to have may not be profitable. We'll talk more about these later but keep all three qualities in mind as you begin to search for possible products.

    To start, you might want to wander through your local campus store to see what products are available (and missing) and at what price. Or, browse the Internet for campus products. Be sure to check your institutional instructions on whether you can compete with other campus providers of goods.

TEAM TROUBLESHOOTING

Problem	Response
No one is leading.	• Rotate the facilitator role each week.
We're not getting anything done. Our meetings are a waste of time.	• Be sure someone is designated to keep the team on task and someone is facilitating discussion. • Set a time limit for the meeting.
One person is dominating the discussion and decision making.	• Practice gate keeping—invite quiet or uninvolved members to speak • Raise the issue in a non-judgmental manner. • Abandon blame and criticism; focus on the greater likelihood of team success when everyone is involved and heard.
We can't seem to agree.	• Consider disagreement as a positive quality—team members feel comfortable speaking up with one another and it provides a chance to work together even better through honest discussion • If the disagreement is dysfunctional—if it is hurting feelings and alienating team members—talk about it as a group process issue; avoid judging and blaming. Listen to each another, consider alternate viewpoints, acknowledge feelings, reach a workable solution, and talk about how you can keep communication channels open. • Avoid owning ideas and letting your ego get tied up with whether an idea is accepted or rejected.
We can't come up with any good ideas.	• Try to identify the reason ideas aren't coming forth—is it apathy, not understanding the task, not understanding the market, or the approach to creativity that is not working? • See time pressure as stimulating creative rather than stifling it. • Think of another event that is familiar and similar to what you are experiencing—perhaps how a coach dealt with an athletic team that was losing the first half of a game or season, or how you loosened a rusty nut from a bolt, or how you solve a math problem.
Only a few of us are doing everything on the team.	• Reiterate mutual team commitments and principles, and the vision of an effective team generated at the beginning of Venture Out • Decide if it's an ability or motivation issue—if motivation, communicate what's at stake and that the help of all is needed; if it's ability, ask the team member what they need to complete the task. • Avoid shouldering too much of the task—others may participate even less if they know someone else is going to do the work for them.
We're constantly behind.	• Build in a time buffer by setting deadlines ahead of the time it's due, then work hard to meet the deadline. • Look ahead so you can see what tasks are next. • Break up big tasks into components you can manage each day.

TIPS FOR WRITING A MISSION STATEMENT

Mission Statements are critical for keeping organizations on track. They define the organization's purpose, business, and values. Although there are many ways to write a mission statement, consider a simple 3-step process for your Venture Out team.[3]

Purpose

The purpose portion of the mission statement tells what your team wants to accomplish: Why does your team exist? What is the ultimate result of your work? Purpose statements usually include two phrases:

- A change in status, such as to increase, decrease, prevent, eliminate
- Identification of a problem or condition to be changed

An example of a purpose statement is "to eliminate homelessness." In defining purpose, it is essential to focus on outcomes and results rather than methods: How is the world going to be different? What is going to change? Thus, the purpose of a mental health counseling agency would never be simply "to provide counseling services" since that describes a method rather than a result. Rather, the purpose might be "to improve the quality of life" for its clients. Similarly, a Venture Out team's purpose wouldn't be an instrumental goal such as "to make an A" or "sell a lot," but a higher goal which states your reason for being.

Business

This part of the mission statement refers to the activities which you will pursue to fulfill your team purpose. Specifically, you must answer, "What activity are we going to do to accomplish our purpose?" For example, there are many ways to work on the problem of homelessness:

- construct housing for homeless individuals
- educate the public and advocate for public policy changes
- provide job training for the homeless

Each of these is a different activity, but they represent different means of achieving the same purpose. Business statements often include the verb "to provide" or link a purpose statement with the words "by" or "through." For example: "To eliminate homelessness by providing job training to homeless individuals."

---

[3] Heidi Sorensen, *Tips for Writing a Mission Statement, 1998*. Adapted with permission from the Alliance for Nonprofit Management, www.allianceonline.org.

Values

Values are beliefs that team members hold and practice together. The values guide your team's members in performing their work. Specifically, you should ask, "What are the basic beliefs that we share as a team?" Examples of values include commitment to:

- excellent customer service
- innovation and creativity
- honesty and integrity

The Writing Process

Groups are good at many things, but wordsmithing is generally not one of them. Discuss your purpose, business, and values and then let one or two individuals draft and redraft the wording before submitting a reworked version for the group to evaluate. Circulate the draft mission statement until team members find it to be a motivating and accurate guide for your activities.

Examples

A few statements (some better than others) from past Venture Out teams are:

- Our mission is to serve the university community by delivering a product that upholds all policies and services, understood and valued by faculty, staff, and students
- Thirst for Compassion strives to captivate the marketplace by providing a quality product that will generate funds and awareness for Compassion International
- To work together as an effective team and produce, market and distribute a desirable product while incorporating values and leadership
- Promote school spirit at an affordable price broadening our knowledge of the many aspects of business
- Team Impressions exists to present a quality product at a competitive price to the student market by working together to benefit Habitat for Humanity
- Our mission is to sell tee-shirts to the students of our university in order to raise awareness and money for the American Cancer Society

TASK 3: ORGANIZING

"Don't agonize. Organize."

~ *Florynce R. Kennedy*

OVERVIEW

Today, the focus is on sub-dividing your company into three groups:

- Consider your market (MARP facilitates TEAM discussion)

- Generate possible products, suppliers, and beneficiaries (MKTG leads TEAM discussion)

- Decide upon the legal status of your company (MGMT facilitates TEAM discussion)

- Complete government form(s) to register your business (if applicable) (MGMT)

- Plan a photo shoot (TEAM)

- Homework: Bring your product, beneficiary, and supplier ideas next week! (TEAM)

- Homework: Read "Participative Premises" (TEAM)

DETAILS

1. Consider your market (MARP facilitates TEAM discussion)

    Individuals new to business sometimes believe that everyone will like a product as well as they do. Or, they assume that if a product is new or cheap, customers will buy it. But if you think about your own behavior as a consumer, you'll realize that you pass by innovative, attractive, well priced products all the time and that good friends who have a lot in common are often drawn to different items on a restaurant menu.

    You probably can't help thinking about possible products at this stage of Venture Out. That's okay to do. In fact, it's good that you're noticing and thinking. But deciding on a product before you think carefully about the market segment you are selling to can cause you to overlook winning products, or worse, set your mind on a product that won't sell because of customer tastes, competition, product design, or pricing. Although there are almost always surprises in sales, businesses nearly always do better when they think of the market first.

Begin by segmenting the entire market available. (Your instructor may limit you to only students, anyone on campus, or other groups. Ask if you're uncertain about the market boundaries.) Then, think about the segments that you're most likely to sell to successfully.

In a real business venture, you'd gather all kinds of data on your target market and your competitors. But since your time and resources are limited, you can get a good start by pooling perceptions within your group. You're just starting your thinking here and you want to remain flexible and creative, so don't try to nail down too much detail. Begin thinking about market segments, your competitors, profit margins, and possible target markets. Here are some specific questions to prompt thought and discussion:

Market Segmentation

- What segments exist within your total market? Consider different ways you can divide the market, such as by age, sororities and fraternities, clubs, geographic origins, majors, marital status, campus events, or other characteristics. Be creative and brainstorm.

- Now, how can you evaluate and compare the segments you've identified? Consider their size, buying power, openness or connection to your team, etc.

Competition

- What general competitors do you need to be aware of as you consider products? Consider on- and off-campus competition, other Venture Out teams, and substitute products. Are markets relatively efficient with little room for your product, or is there room to enter the market and be successful? There are only so many disposable dollars to go around so you want to end up with an attractive product and a promotional strategy that will attract those scarce dollars. (A competitive analysis is a bit early at this stage because you probably don't have a product identified. Being generally aware of competitors in the marketplace can be healthy, however.)

- How do you anticipate your competitors will respond to your entrance into the market? Is there any way to gain an advantage over the competition, such as via pre-selling, product benefits, market access, low cost, appeal of the beneficiary you will choose, etc.?

Profit Margin

- What profit margin range should you consider as you evaluate possible products? The lower the profit margin, the more products you'll need to sell. Simply stated, to make $100 of profit with a product having a $5 profit margin means you'll have to sell 20 items. To make the same profit with a 25¢ margin you'll have to sell 400 items. If you price your product too high, however, your market may not buy it.

Based on your answers to these questions, which market segments seem promising? What about profit margin range or products or markets to avoid based on your thoughts about competitors?

2. Generate possible products, suppliers, and beneficiaries (MKTG facilitates TEAM discussion)

If you want to now, take a few moments to brainstorm possible products. Don't criticize or inhibit any idea offered. There will be time to critique later. For now, think creatively and broadly, using these or other techniques:

- Think of specific products you've seen elsewhere but not on your campus
- Consider past Venture Out products (if you know of some) that have been successful
- Think about your most promising market segments—what might they need or want?
- Look at promotional product catalogs on the Internet retail sites

Product Guidelines

Keep in mind these guidelines regarding product selection:

- Because of their risk or other factors, your instructor may discourage or not allow you to sell services (e.g., car washes or massages) or fund-raising (e.g., raffle tickets); check with them if you're unsure
- Selling products which compete directly with campus store products may be off limits; again ask the instructor
- Products should be consistent with institutional culture, ethics, and social responsibility
- Consider seasonality during selling—tee-shirts may not sell well in cold weather and demand for sports items may drop off in off-season
- If you want to use a university logo on your product, whether names, slogans, letters, or a mascot, consult with your instructor. Colleges and universities want to guard their brands carefully, just as companies do. Most don't allow logos to be modified and some don't want them used at all

Suppliers

- A local supplier can solve a lot of problems for you. Even though you have to pay sales tax and sometimes a higher price, local suppliers are often fast and if there's a problem, you can talk with them face-to-face. Plus, you'll be contributing to the local economy.

- Sometimes an Internet supplier or suppliers located elsewhere can get a product you can't order locally, but if you go with one, proceed with care and get all your specifics in writing (e.g., the price including any charges for special printing, taxes, shipping—the delivery time, minimum order quantities, etc.).

- Inspect the goods. If available, examine a sample of the product. Suppliers typically can't custom print a sample but sometimes they have fabric swatches or samples they can provide. Pictures on the Internet or in a catalog don't always convey qualities like thickness, color, feel, and size.

3. Decide upon the legal status of your company (MGMT facilitates TEAM discussion)

    One thing a company must decide is what type of legal status they want to have. Consult your textbook or the Internet on various legal structures and their advantages and disadvantages, and decide which one best fits your organization. Some forms you might want to consider would be general partnership (GP), limited partnership (LP), limited liability company (LLC), professional corporation (PC), S-Corporation, C-Corporation, or non-profit corporation.

4. Complete government form(s) to register your business (if applicable) (MGMT)

    Although you don't need to actually register your team as a business in your city, county, or state or with the US Internal Revenue Service (IRS), your instructor may want you to know about this process and complete one or more forms so you can know how it's done. Consult with him or her if you are unsure of this requirement.

5. Plan a photo shoot (TEAM)

    Plan a photo shoot that could be made before Task 6. Look around this week and choose just the right venue for your company. If you have a preference on dress, be sure to agree ahead of time and remind everyone through your team communication system. You'll need a:

    - Company photo (get every team member in the photo if possible)
    - Photo of each group (MKTG, etc.)

6. Homework: Bring product, beneficiary, and supplier ideas next week (TEAM)

    Keep your eyes open for sure fire products and suppliers, and worthy beneficiaries.

7. Homework: Read "Participative Premises" (TEAM) – do this before the next task

---

PARTICIPATIVE LEADERSHIP
Max DePree

What is it most of us really want from work? We would like to find the most effective, most productive, most rewarding way of working together. We would like a work process and relationships that meet our personal needs for belonging, for contributing, for meaningful work, for the opportunity to make a commitment, for the opportunity to grow and be at least reasonably in control of our own destinies. Finally, we'd like someone to say "Thank you!"

Participative management arises out of the heart and out of a personal philosophy about people. Effective influencing and understanding spring largely from healthy relationships among the members of the group. Leaders need to foster environments and work processes within which people can develop high-quality relationships with each other, with the group with which we work, and with our clients and customers.

How does one approach the problem of turning the ideals about relationships into reality? I would propose five steps as a starting point.

Respect people. Understanding the diversity of their gifts enables us to begin taking the crucial step of trusting each other. It also enables us to begin to think in a new way about the strengths of others. True participation and enlightened leadership allow these gifts to be expressed in different ways at different times.

Understand that what we believe precedes policy and practice. It seems to me that our value system and world view should be as closely integrated into our work lives as they are integrated into our lives with our families, churches, and other activities and groups. Style is merely a consequence of what we believe, of what is in our hearts.

Agree on the rights of work. Each of us, no matter what our rank in the hierarchy, has the same rights: to be needed, to be involved, to have a covenantal relationship, to understand the corporation, to affect our destiny, to be accountable, to appeal, to make a commitment.

Understand the respective role and relationship of contractual agreements and covenants. Contractual relationships cover such things as compensation, benefits, timetables, etc. Covenantal relationships enable corporations and institutions to be hospitable to the unusual person and to unusual ideas.

Understand that relationships count more than structure. Structures do not have anything to do with trust. People build trust.

Finally, one question: **Would you rather work as a part of an outstanding group or be a part of a group of outstanding individuals?**

Excerpted and adapted from Max DePree, *Leadership is an Art*, New York: Dell, 1989, pp. 23-29.

TASK 4: EXPLORING

"I can see the time when every city will have one."

~One American mayor's reaction upon hearing about the invention of the telephone

OVERVIEW

- Discuss possible products and suppliers (TEAM)
- Identify possible beneficiaries (TEAM)
- Estimate tentative group budgets (TEAM)
- Company and group photo shoot (MGMT)
- Team check (TEAM)
- Homework: Prepare a budget scenario worksheet (FINA)

DETAILS

1. Discuss possible products and suppliers (TEAM)

   Pool your ideas of possible products and try to narrow your top choices to two or three which fit the target market and product selection criteria you discussed in the last task. If you aren't ready to narrow the field, assign team members to research products this week so you can select a product quickly and wisely next week.

   Remember that some products may be great ideas and would be in demand, but they may be too expensive to yield an adequate profit margin. To avoid this, it's smart to obtain pricing estimates as you evaluate potential products.

2. Identify possible beneficiaries (TEAM)

   Your instructor may specify that profits be donated to a common beneficiary or scholarship fund. But if you are donating your profits to a beneficiary of your choice, consider questions such as:

- What type of services does the beneficiary provide (e.g., poverty, education, health, etc.)?

- Who is their target population (e.g., children, elderly)?

- How are they funded?

To give everyone a chance to participate, you might brainstorm a list of possible beneficiaries and then discuss the list together. You could select a beneficiary today if your team is ready, or make assignments to gather more information and choose during the next task. You may wish to include a brochure, Web page printout, or a paragraph of basic information about the beneficiary, along with a mailing address in your business plan.

3. Estimate tentative group budgets (TEAM)

Each group should estimate a lean but adequate budget to operate effectively. Itemize your needs and list the cost of each. Give your budget estimate to the FINA group today so they can assimilate them into a single budget. Items that cannot be included in the budget are:

- Excessive contingency funds—although building in a buffer for unexpected expenses is often reasonable, excessive slush funds can simply be an excuse for sloppy budgeting. Since budgeting uncertainties in Venture Out expenses are minimal, keep your budget lean.

- Company food or goodies—sorry, but you'll need to use external funds if you give awards to team members for their sales or want to buy food for outside meetings. If a business wants to donate a gift certificate or goodie for your team, that's fine. Most teams will forgo these types of rewards, even though they may be effective practices in some businesses.

No company can be subsidized—no friend or family member can donate money, labor, or materials to offset costs in your project. Venture Out is a business simulation founded on business principles rather than a fundraiser built on donations. If a supplier wishes to provide a product at wholesale prices, that's okay—they just can't distort the market by excessively underwriting your company.

In a start-up, you want to have deep enough resources that you can survive early months when your costs may be mounting and your sales are still building. But a key to succeeding in a new venture start-up is to manage your costs to be as lean as possible. The way you could practice that principle is to keep your costs to a minimum, maximize your profit potential, and request the smallest loan needed to achieve your goals. The smaller the loan, the less you'll have to repay.

4. Company and group photo shoot (MGMT)

   Take your company photos today or stay on track with a plan for shooting them soon.

5. Team check (TEAM)

   Today's a good day to pause and assess your team's effectiveness. Conclude today by honestly discussing the following questions:

   - What have we done well as a team?

   - What's keeping us as a team from functioning even better?

   - What action could we take to enhance our team performance?

   Avoid blaming or accusing other team members. If there are serious performance issues—such as some members are working hard but others are not—recall your agreed upon accountability principles and commit to an action plan that will address these problems. Communicate honestly, assertively, and tactfully. Involve your coach and/or instructor if needed. Your instructor may have a procedure for addressing a team member who has not been involved. If you want to know more, just ask.

6. Homework: Prepare a budget scenario worksheet (FINA)

   After receiving each group's budget, consolidate these into a budget scenario worksheet, keeping the itemized listings for each group so you can see all the budget detail. An example is provided below. To help your team contrast various products at different price points, create your worksheet with formulas so you can see the effect of different prices and costs on your net profit.

   The FINA group should insure sound team financial decisions are made so don't accept budgets as given—question any items which you believe are unnecessary or excessive or inadequate before consolidating them into the team budget. In two weeks you'll need to present a draft budget to the company. An example of a budget is also given on the following pages.

BUDGET SCENARIO WORKSHEET EXAMPLE

To plan effectively, businesses need to estimate expenses and revenues as accurately as possible. Venture Out budgets are simple and easy to build once you have itemized your expenses and decided on your product and pricing. Here's an example of a worksheet which you can build in Microsoft Office Excel:

Team Wildcat Budget Scenario Worksheet					
Category	Item	Cost/Price Per Item	Number of Items	Total
INCOME				
Sales	Tee-shirts	$ 12.00	74	$ 888.00
Total				$ 888.00
EXPENSES				
Cost of Goods Sold	Tee-shirts	$ 5.65	74	$ 418.10
Marketing	Sample product	$ 6.95	1	$ 6.95
Marketing	Poster board	$ 0.45	3	$ 1.35
Administration	Annual report & business plan notebooks	$ 1.69	4	$ 6.76
Total				$ 433.16
NET PROFIT				$ 454.84

If you use formulas to create the cells in the total column, you can insert different numbers in the cells highlighted above; the totals will update automatically. You may not be familiar with putting positives (income) and negatives (expenses) in the same column but this is a format commonly used when an accountant prepares an Income Statement. Notice that the income is listed first and expenses, second. You can calculate net profit by subtracting expenses from income.

TASK 5: RESEARCHING

"It is a capital mistake to theorize before one has data. Insensibly one begins to twist facts to suit theories, instead of theories to suit facts."

~ Sir Arthur Conan Doyle

OVERVIEW

- Decide on a beneficiary (TEAM)
- Design your market research survey and gather results (TEAM)
- Homework: Tabulate the research results and make recommendations (MARP and FINA)
- Homework: Begin assembling items for your business plan (MGMT)

DETAILS

1. Decide on a beneficiary (TEAM)

   If you are choosing beneficiaries by team and you haven't done so already, decide upon a beneficiary today.

2. Design your market research survey and gather results (TEAM)

   One way entrepreneurs and businesses manage risk is to survey what potential customers think of your product. Businesses sometimes collect quick product impressions and at other times, detailed assessments. You'll want to learn how to gather just the right amount of data and ask the right kinds of questions to get feedback which helps you make good business decisions.

   The main activity between this task and the next one is to design a survey, collect data, and tabulate the results so you decide which product to sell and at what price. Lots of businesses think they've nailed their products and pricing. But you just have to look down a local business district to find stores and companies that didn't make it after just a few months (and thousands or millions of dollars) in business. Regardless of what you think about your product, you want to know what customers think. You'll want to show the Loan Review Board that you have gathered and used valid and reliable data from your target market in deciding upon your product, its price, and your promotional strategy.

Today, you'll want to do the following:

Inside class:

- Construct a brief survey (3-6 questions) dealing with possible pricing and product design options. Include enough variety (e.g., two products, two or three logo designs, two or three colors, etc.) so that you're assured at least one product that will work in your business plan.

- If needed, include a clear product graphic to insure that respondents have an accurate image of your product. Colors, fonts, size and placement of wording—these and other important product design characteristics should be communicated to respondents.

- If you anticipate ordering a product that comes in several sizes, be sure to ask respondents what size they wear. This isn't to obligate them to buy, but so you'll know how much of your market wears various sizes.

- Ask your instructor to review and approve the survey. (This is important. Your instructor can insure that you are asking questions that will yield valid and reliable data.)

For additional recommendations on survey wording, see the "Designing Survey Questions" recommendations below and the example at the end of this task.

Outside of class and before the next Venture Out task:

- Type and duplicate the survey.

- Distribute the survey to 30-60 individuals in your target market. Survey professionally; don't hassle students; obtain permission to distribute surveys if required. You may receive more accurate data and a higher response rate if you distribute and collect printed surveys than if you distribute them electronically.

- Be sure the MARP group receives the surveys in time to tabulate the results so you can make product decisions during the Task 6.

The entire team should help design the survey and gather the results.

DESIGNING SURVEY QUESTIONS

Asking the right questions can guide you toward designing a successful product and making sales a breeze.

Avoid double-barreled questions because respondents may feel differently about two attributes. For example, don't ask:

"How much do you like the color and shape of this product?"

Avoid asking only questions that don't tell you whether respondents would purchase the product. For example:

"Which of these three products do you like best?"

"Rank these products from best to worst."

Instead, ask:

"How likely would you be to purchase this product?"

"What is the most you would pay for this product?"

"What t-shirt sizes do you generally buy for yourself?"

Feel free to ask about any extra items, such as:

"What could we change to make this product more appealing?"

"How many of these are you likely to buy?"

...anything to help you understand what the target market wants.

3. Homework: Tabulate the research results and make recommendations (MARP and FINA)

The MARP group should tabulate the results before your next team meeting. You might put the data in a Microsoft Excel spreadsheet and generate pie charts or bar charts to illustrate the results graphically. The MARP group may want to work with the budget spreadsheet designed by the FINA members so you can test various scenarios on product price points and number of products to order. Finally, based on your analysis, be prepared to offer the TEAM your recommendations on which product (including designs, colors, sizes, etc.) and price to choose, and why.

4. Homework: Begin assembling your business plan (MGMT)

Next week, you'll need to assemble a business plan for the Loan Review Board. Look ahead at the Business Plan Checklist in Task 6, start collecting any items you can, and begin assembling the plan. It may be best to designate one place (e.g., Google Docs or Microsoft Groove) or one person to coordinate this collection process. If you start from scratch next week, you'll be pressed for time and may struggle to produce a professional report. Remember, judges will be reviewing the plan you create. If you don't have all the information you need yet, you can create a shell into which you can drop content and details when they become available. Business plans may be assembled in a variety of software packages but you might try Microsoft Word or Microsoft Publisher.

SURVEY EXAMPLE

Venture Out Product Survey

There's no obligation to purchase anything, we just need your feedback for a business class. Could you respond to a few questions?

~ Irish Tee-shirt ~   ~ Wildcat Tee-shirt ~   ~ Wildcat Baseball Tee-shirt ~

1. **If offered at a reasonable price, how likely would you be to purchase:**
   (circle one number on each line)

	I Would Not Buy It		I Might Buy It		I Would Buy It
A. Irish tee-shirt	1	2	3	4	5
B. Wildcat tee-shirt	1	2	3	4	5
C. Wildcat baseball shirt	1	2	3	4	5

2. **What is the highest price you would pay for:**
   (circle one number on each line)

A. Irish tee-shirt	$10	$11	$12	$13	$14	$15
B. Wildcat tee-shirt	$10	$11	$12	$13	$14	$15
C. Wildcat baseball shirt	$12	$13	$14	$15	$16	$17

3. **Rank these tee-shirt colors according to your preference:**
   (write in 1 for first choice, 2 for second choice, 3 for third choice, and 4 for fourth choice)

   ___ Grey
   ___ Black
   ___ White
   ___ Medium blue

4. **When you purchase a tee-shirt for yourself, what size do you usually buy?**
   (circle one or more)

   S   M   L   XL   XXL   XXXL

   Thank you!

TASK 6: PROPOSING

"Effective management always means asking the right questions."

~ Robert Heller

OVERVIEW

- Review market research and recommendations from MARP and choose a product and supplier (TEAM)

- Get approval of your product from your instructor (TEAM)

- Verify the trustworthiness of your supplier (MARP)

- Approve a company budget (TEAM; data and recommendations provided by FINA)

- Choose a company name (TEAM)

- Arrange a time to present your business plan to the Loan Review Board (TEAM)

- Homework: Prepare your business plan (MGMT)

DETAILS

Things are about to get busy! Work efficiently but make wise choices—your success depends in large measure upon the care of your business decision making, teamwork, and execution!

1. Review market research and recommendations from MARP and choose a product and supplier (TEAM)

    The MARP group should present a summary of the market research results, their recommendations for the product and its design, pricing, and the amount of product to order. You may also want to discuss where will be the best locations to sell your product and if you want to consider any special way of promoting it. Keeping it simple and selling by word-of-mouth generally works well, but you might have some creative ideas too. The group should be prepared to respond to questions and provide details of the data if requested by team members. Consider if you will pre-sell or bundle (e.g. 1 for $6 or 2 for $10). Having a solid basic plan is more important than a detailed complicated plan.

It's important that the team reach consensus on the product decision. Disagreement within teams is common and can keep you from accepting a product that may fail in the marketplace. If team members have concerns, hear them out and consider them with an open mind. If the team goes with a product that you're not behind, and your concerns have been voiced and heard, it may be time to accept the decision of the team and give it your full support.

Regarding a supplier, be sure you have an estimate in writing with all costs listed. For example, is there a set-up fee for printing? Tax? Shipping? Extra cost for large sizes or colors? You might also want to clarify what the return policy is before you order.

2. Get approval on your product from your instructor (TEAM)

    Before proceeding, be sure to get an okay on your product choice from your instructor. He or she will want to insure that it is consistent with the values and mission of your institution and that it is of reasonable risk for the team to undertake.

3. Verify the trustworthiness of your supplier (MARP)

    A useful phrase in business transactions is "due diligence." It simply means investigating details and references carefully. It's always wise to do due diligence when it comes to entering into business with someone. One way to do this with a supplier is to check with the Better Business Bureau (BBB). Just check their Web site (www.bbb.org) for your supplier.

    A clear record with the BBB doesn't guarantee you won't have delays or hassles, but it is a minimal check for Venture Out. If you are hesitant, contact the supplier or go with a different one, even if your cost is higher. If a BBB statement is available for your supplier, print a copy for your business plan. If a report is unavailable, you might ask your supplier for references or accept a personal referral from someone who has done business with them. The main point is to insure that your supplier is dependable.

4. Approve a company budget (TEAM; data and recommendations provided by FINA)

    The FINA group should present a company budget based on the submitted budgets of the various groups. Questions and discussion of the budget should be encouraged, with possible changes being made based on the discussion. Remember…running lean means less debt to overcome. Be sure to check any grading requirements for profit in your syllabus or in instructions from your instructor.

5. Choose a company name (TEAM)

   It's time to come up with a company name. You can go with a name that reflects the group's composition and spirit, such as:

   - Six Guys and a Girl
   - The Great-8
   - Team Xtreme
   - Lucky Seven

   Many teams choose a name that reflects their product and/or beneficiary, such as:

   - Sockitoya (socks)
   - The Cat in the Hat (as in...a Wildcat (school mascot) and a toboggan)
   - Bands "R" Us (armbands)
   - This Little Light (keychain flashlight)

   Be creative!

6. Arrange a time to present your business plan to the Loan Review Board (TEAM)

   If your instructor presents them to you today, be sure to:

   - Sign up for a time to meet with the Loan Review Board next week
   - Choose 3 or more team members to present your plan to the Loan Review Board

7. Homework: Prepare your business plan for the Loan Review Board (MGMT)

The team members representing the company should meet with the MGMT group who is charged with assembling a professional, 10-17 page business plan for the Loan Review Board. This will take some time and it's an important document so start working on it now. Schedule your work so you allow enough time for the entire team to review the plan. The more eyes, the more chance you'll catch errors. Try to present a perfect professional plan with a winning business strategy, and hit a home run with the Loan Review Board.

Your instructor will tell you how much time you will have to present your plan and what else will happen during the presentation. Usually, the board will ask questions about plan details. Bring 3 copies of your plan for the Loan Review Board judges. Incorporate any graphics, photos, charts, appendices, and graphic layout you wish but insure that they sell your plan rather than simply add bulk. Pay special attention to the visual layout of your plan—you want it to be comprehended at a glance. Avoid long paragraphs; use bullets, headings, and tables when they help. Microsoft Office and Microsoft Publisher offer several document styles which you can choose from or you can create your own.

Your business plan must contain the following items in the order presented. You can add other elements that help sell your business but keep them to a minimum. An example plan follows the checklist:

BUSINESS PLAN CHECKLIST[4]

Cover Page {1 page}

❑ Name of your company

❑ Contact information – Include an address, email, and phone number of the report editor or management group member or other appropriate team member

❑ Date the report was completed

❑ Copy – Often copies of the report are numbered so you can keep track of who has what copy; these are generally documents you want to keep confidential. Something like "Copy 1 of 3" and so forth. (Tip: Be sure to change the number for each copy.)

❑ At the bottom, add this statement: "This business plan has been submitted on a confidential basis solely for the benefit of qualified investors and is not for use by any other persons. Do not copy, fax, reproduce, or distribute without permission."

Table of Contents {1 page}

List the major headings (indicated by • in the Business Plan Checklist) and individual items in your appendix (if relevant) [Tip: Be sure to add page numbers to your pages.]

Executive Summary {about 1 page}

[Tip: Hook the investor's attention so they want to read more; you can use the following as headings or bullets or include the content in a letter to potential

---

[4] Everything you need to prepare your Venture Out business plan is described in this manual. If you want to read more about business plans, an excellent how-to manual is: Jeffry A. Timmons, Andrew Zacharakis, and Stephen Spinelli, *Business Plans that Work* (New York: McGraw-Hill, 2004).

investors, but try to keep it to one page. The elements should be self-explanatory, easy to read at a glance, and flow, but be crisply worded.]

❑ Introduction – State your company's name and mission statement

❑ Opportunity – Briefly describe the opportunity or opening in the marketplace for your product. Why is there a need for your product? Consider things such as seasonality, unique designs, affinity toward your beneficiary, and other factors.

❑ Business Concept – In a short paragraph, describe your product; include one or two small graphics so the reader can visualize your company's product.

❑ Industry Overview – Briefly describe your competition; consider direct competitors as well as substitute products. Who sells products that might compete with yours?

❑ Competitive Advantage – Briefly describe or list why your product is uniquely better than anything else on the market. Consider its design, quality, price, beneficiary, or other characteristics that distinguish it above competing products.

❑ Team – List the names of your team members and one characteristic about each person (e.g., their major or experience) that shows their value to the venture. Keep it brief.

❑ Financial Highlights – In a small table, show your projected revenue (the money you anticipate attracting through sales), cost of goods sold, gross profit (revenue minus COGS), other expenses, and your net earnings (revenue minus operating expenses). You'll be able to use this table again in the financial section of the plan.

❑ Status and Offering – State your requested loan amount.

❑ Beneficiary – In a sentence, state what beneficiary your profits will go toward and what they do.

Market Analysis and Marketing Plan {2 to 4 pages, depending on graphics}

❑ Market Research – Summarize pertinent market research findings using pie charts and/or bar graphs—whichever illustrates the data best—and enough description to explain the question or data. State the number of individuals surveyed. [Tip: Be sure your charts and graphs are clearly titled and the axes or segments are appropriately labeled.]

❑ Target Market – Briefly describe your general market (e.g., the students at your school) and/or any specific segment(s) you are targeting. Briefly describe the segment, including its size and any differentiating characteristics, for example: "Our target market is a 125-member Greek fraternity." [Tip: Insure that your product design, sales and advertising, and pricing all fit your target market.]

❑ Product – Describe any product details which may not have been included in the Executive Summary. If needed, include a larger product photo or enlargement of the design—the point is to insure the investor has a clear sense of your product. [Tip: Bring a sample to the Loan Review Board meeting if you have one.]

❑ Supplier — Include a sentence or two about your supplier, giving their name and location and any other information that you believe is helpful, such as their industry or product line, how long they have been in business, and/or why you chose them.

❑ Price – Briefly describe your pricing strategy, including the price you are going to charge, prices of competing products, and why your "price point" (the price you are charging) gives you a competitive advantage or fits your target market. [Tip: Offering the lowest price is one strategy but there are others, such as offering more value—a better quality or unique product—at a higher price.]

❑ Promotion and Distribution – Include any relevant information on advertising and sales tactics, stating where you anticipate most of your selling to occur (e.g., informally in residents halls, at a table in the student union or campus center, at basketball games, etc.) and any special promotional tactics such as bundling items so customers receive a reduced price if they buy several, pre-selling to customers before the product arrives, wearing your product, advertising in the school newspaper, sales tactics, etc. Of course, you'll want to avoid promotional tactics that violate school policies or reflect poorly on Venture Out. [Tip: The goal is not to be elaborate, outlandish, or unique, but to be effective. A simple and informal promotional strategy may be fine unless you face considerable competition or your target market doesn't know you.]

❑ Sales Forecast – Include a table and brief description which projects your sales by week during the sales period (see your syllabus or ask your instructor if you are unsure of the length of your sales period). Include for each week the sales in units and dollars, cumulative sales in units and dollars, number of people selling, and sales per salesperson in units.

Financial Plan {1 page}

State these amounts with minimal or no description. (Tip: Be sure your calculations are accurate and be prepared to describe how you arrived at the numbers to the Loan Review Board if they ask.)

❑ Budget – List all the expenses in your budget from your Budget Scenario Worksheet (Task 4).

- ❏ Pro Forma Income Statement – You've already prepared this one. Just copy your financial highlights chart from the Executive Summary. A pro forma statement shows anticipated rather than actual financial performance. (Tip: The information on this chart should be consistent with all other figures and charts in your plan.)

- ❏ Unit Cost – Your unit cost is how much you are paying for each item of product. Include all direct costs for your product such as sales tax, shipping and handling, set-up charges for custom screen printing.

    Example: If you are paying $487.16 for 40 umbrellas, including tax and shipping, your unit cost would be $487.16/40 = $12.18.

- ❏ Breakeven – The breakeven point is simply the number of products you must sell to be out of debt and begin earning a profit. Calculating breakeven is easy in Venture Out because generally all costs are one-time expenses. If this is true in your case, simply divide your total costs (e.g., your product along with any shipping and sales tax, any promotional materials or binders, etc., but not your loan amount) by the price you are charging for a single unit of your product. The number that remains is the "breakeven."

    Example: If your total expenses equal $427 and you are going to sell reusable water bottles for $8 each, your breakeven is 54.

- ❏ Profit Margin – This financial ratio indicates the percent of profit made from your sales. It's simply total projected profit divided by total projected sales.

    Example: If your projected sales = $891, and your projected profit = $347, your profit margin is $347/$891 = 38.94%.

- ❏ Requested Loan – State the loan amount you are requesting (Tip: It's okay to round up to the nearest dollar when you calculate the total needed. Be sure you do not exceed the maximum specified by your instructor, however.)

Team {1 page}

- ❏ Organization Chart – Organizations often utilize organization charts to insure clear reporting relationships and show groupings of employees. Small, entrepreneurial firms usually rely on informal structures, and yours is likely to be even simpler and flatter since you may not have any hierarchy on the team. But to gain some experience with organization charts, draw one and insert it here showing the team members by name. The team—the depth and breadth of experience and their ability to work together—is often of critical importance to investors. (Tip: You can make an organization chart in Microsoft PowerPoint and import it into your business plan.)

Beneficiary *(if relevant) {1 page or less}*

- ❑ Name and Information – Give the name and location of your beneficiary, and a brief description of their activities, and (if relevant) why you chose them.

Repayment Agreement *{1 page}*

- ❑ Conclude your business plan with the following statement followed by signature lines, and have every employee sign it:

   "We pledge to share an equal portion of paying back the loan and/or any additional expenses incurred by the team if the company is not profitable, whether due to inadequate sales to cover expenses and/or the misappropriate of funds. The total debt will be divided equally across all company employees."

Appendix *{1 to 5 pages}*

Include only if you have one or more of the items below:

- ❑ Survey – Include a blank copy of your market research survey form
- ❑ Better Business Bureau Endorsement – If you found an evaluation of your supplier on the BBB Web site, print it out and include it here.
- ❑ Contracts – If you are working with a single customer—such as a campus club or organization—you should have a contract with them insuring they are going to purchase your product. Include it here.
- ❑ Approvals – If you are using an official school logo or other copyrighted or trademarked material, include appropriate permissions.
- ❑ Business Registration – If your instructor wants you to complete a state, county, or municipal business registration form, include it here.

An example of a Venture Out business plan follows these instructions. It's a good one but feel free to use your own style and see if you can make yours even better!

Team Harold's Business Plan

Contact:

ACU Box 10000
Abilene, TX 79699
325-677-7777
teamharolds@acu.edu

The date is important; in a real venture, you'll likely alter your plan as you keep learning.

Dated: December 1, 2008
Copy: 1 of 3

Be sure to change the copy number on successive copies. Plans are numbered so you can keep your idea confidential.

This business plan has been submitted on a confidential basis solely for the benefit of qualified investors and is not for use by any other persons. Do not copy, fax, reproduce, or distribute without permission.

Table of Contents

Executive Summary. 3

Market Analysis and Marketing Plan
    Market Research. 4
    Target Market. 5
    Product. 5
    Supplier. 5
    Price. 5
    Promotion and Distribution. 6
    Sales Forecast. 6

Financial Plan
    Budget. 7
    Pro Forma Income Statement. 7
    Other Financial Information. 7

Team. 8

Beneficiary. 9

Repayment Agreement 10

Appendix
    Survey. 11
    Better Business Bureau Endorsement 12
    Contracts. 13

> Number your pages so you can help readers locate pages easily

> In your final edit, check to see that your page numbers are correct.

Executive Summary

Introduction
- Team Harold's mission is to provide a sizzling Harold's Barbeque t-shirt for university students, generating proceeds for Special Olympics of Texas.

Opportunity
- Harold's Barbeque is an authentic restaurant in Abilene, Texas with a considerable following among university students. Despite its brand loyalty, Harold's has not been promoted.

Business Concept
- We have developed a colorful tee-shirt displaying the Harold's logo.

Industry Overview
- Tee-shirts range from a low of $8 at discount retailers to $18 at high end stores. Imprinted t-shirts are worn frequently by guys and girls on campus. Unique brands are valued.

Competitive Advantage
- Unique design of popular apparel at a low price

Team
- Rich Blaylock and Michael Eberhardt serve on the management team. Christy Johnson, Kennedy Thomas, and Callie Winegeart head up finance and accounting. Susan Sparks and Zel Milegar coordinate marketing. Our team has experience in retail, sales, and banking.

Financial Highlights

Pro Forma Income Statement		2008
PROJECTED REVENUES		$690.00
Cost of Goods Sold		$454.50
GROSS PROFIT		$235.50
% of Revenues	33%	
Operating Expenses (incl. sales tax)		$7.51
NET EARNINGS		$227.99

Status and Offering
- Team Harold's is not yet funded and is seeking a loan of **$466**.

Beneficiary
- Our profits will be donated to COBA student scholarships and Special Olympics of Texas.

Market Analysis and Marketing Plan

Market Research

- We distributed surveys (see Appendix) to 63 friends, peers, and strangers and asked them seven questions about their product preferences. The information we gathered from this survey confirmed a positive level of interest in this product and directed our decisions for product layout, color, design, and price.

- Over two-thirds of the respondents had eaten at Harold's. The majority preferred a yellow shirt over red. Over 80% would be willing to pay $10 or more for a t-shirt. Most preferred a logo on the front of the shirt and 76% said they might or were very likely to purchase a shirt. About half wear small or medium size.

Have you ever eaten at Harold's Barbeque?

Yes: 71%

No: 29%

How likely would you be to buy a Harold's t-shirt?

Very Likely: 33%

Maybe: 43%

Not likely: 24%

Where would you place Harold's logo on a shirt?

Front: 63%

Back: 37%

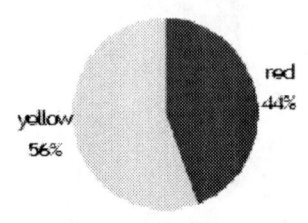

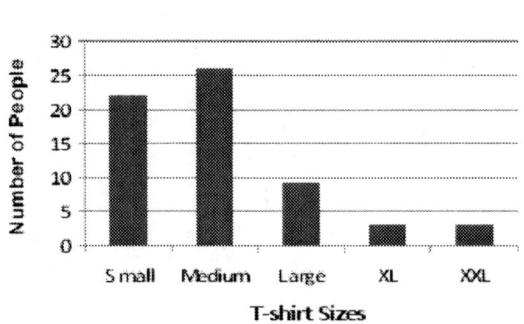

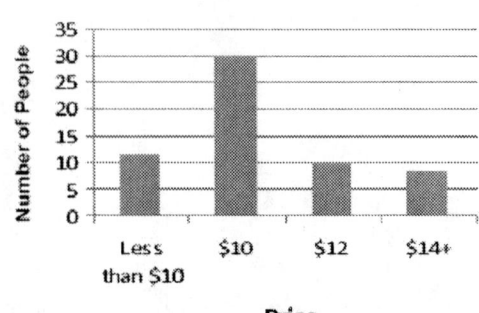

Label and title your graphs and charts.

Market Analysis and Marketing Plan (con't)

Target Market

- Our target market are university students on campus who have eaten at Harold's Barbeque and are a fan of Harold's World Famous Barbeque Sauce.

Product

- Based on loyalty of Harold's customers and the results of the market research survey, we have decided to produce a yellow T-shirt with the Harold's logo on the front, and the phrase "ACU FOR BBQ" on the back. We are ordering 69 t-shirts. An image of our shirt is below:

Supplier

- Excel Screenprinting in Abilene, Texas has existed since 1991. They custom print apparel such as caps, shirts, and sweatshirts. We chose them because of our personal past satisfied experiences with their service.

Price

- We will be selling our t-shirts for $10, as compared to t-shirts in the Campus Store which range from $9.99 to $15.99. We wanted to keep our product price down to maximize the number of buyers since many potential customers we surveyed said that they were not willing to pay over $10. Ten dollars is also an easy amount to work with since customers will not have to dig in their wallet to find quarters or one dollar bills to make change.

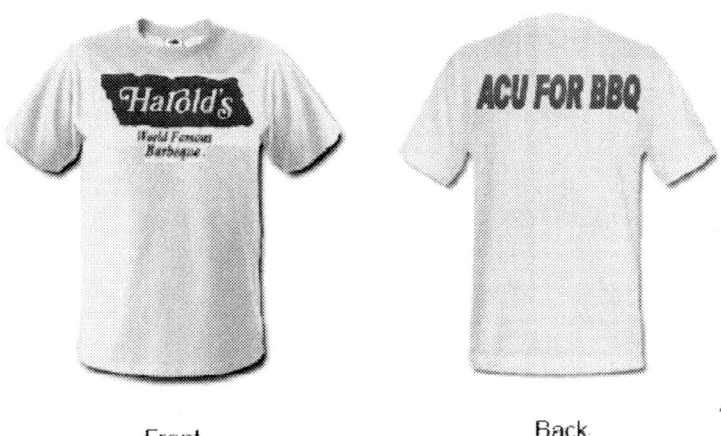

Front   Back

Market Analysis and Marketing Plan (con't)

Promotion and Distribution

- The originality of our product will be our main sales tactic, because Harold's t-shirts have never been made before, and are not sold at his restaurant. If students know that these shirts are a one-time offer, we believe they will be more likely to buy them.
- We will promote shirts by letting potential customers know the profits go to the Special Olympics, and are not for our personal gain. We plan to advertise these shirts by word of mouth as well as by posting notifications to Harold's fan base on Facebook, including the 516-member Harold's Facebook group.
- T-shirts will be sold in the Campus Center as well as through individual sales by each team member. The ideal selling times will be during lunch. Any additional selling times will be dependant on each team member's class schedule.

Sales Forecast

- We believe our product will be in demand and thus are projecting a moderately aggressive sales forecast, as summarized in the table below:

	Sales Forecast				
	Week 1	Week 2	Week 3	Week 4	Week 5
Units	24	18	16	11	0
Cumulative Units	24	42	58	69	69
Sales	$240	$180	$160	$110	$0
Cumulative Sales	$240	$420	$580	$690	$690
Salespeople	6	6	6	6	6
Units/ Salespeople	4	3	2.67	1.83	0

> Use this forecast to motivate and measure your sales performance.

Financial Plan

Budget and Expected Financial Performance

- Our projected expenses consist mostly of our product, with minimal marketing and management expenses. Our margins and projected income are strong.

Budget		
Group	Item	Amount
Marketing	Shirts	$454.50
Marketing	Poster board	$0.41
Management	Folders	$7.10
Finance	Cash box	$3.06
TOTAL		**$465.07**

Pro Forma Income Statement	
	2008
PROJECTED REVENUES	$690.00
Cost of Goods Sold	$454.50
GROSS PROFIT	$235.50
% of Revenues	34%
Operating Expenses	$7.51
NET EARNINGS	$227.99

Check all your numbers carefully. Mistakes raise questions about your conscientiousness with details.

Other Financial Information	
Unit Cost (incl. sales tax and set-up)	$6.59
Breakeven	46 shirts
Profit Margin	32.47%
Requested Loan	**$466.00**

Team Harold's

- **Management**
  - Rich Blaylock
  - Michael Eberhardt
- **Marketing & Production**
  - Susan Sparks
  - Zel Milegar
- **Accounting & Finance**
  - Christy Johnson
  - Kennedy Thomas
  - Callie Winegeart

> Business plans generally tell about the backgrounds of the partners. You can do that if you like or keep it simple.

Beneficiary

Special Olympics Texas is a movement dedicated to providing people with intellectual disabilities an opportunity to achieve. Special Olympics is not just about athletic competitions. The movement is also about working together with others, gaining self-confidence and learning additional skills that make it possible for our athletes to become significant and productive citizens of our communities. Special Olympics really is a growing movement that creates a lasting and positive imprint across virtually every segment of our society and in the hearts of everyone it touches.

As a donor, you can see your gift in action through diverse, year-round volunteer opportunities. Since the Special Olympics program is available in every community, your donation benefits local athletes. And ultimately, your generosity can provide a life-changing experience for individuals with intellectual disabilities well into the future.

Address:

Special Olympics Texas
State Headquarters
7715 Chevy Chase Dr.
Suite 120
Austin, TX 78752

Source: Special Olympics of Texas Web site

Repayment Agreement

We pledge to share an equal portion of paying back the loan and/or any additional expenses incurred by the team if the company is not profitable, whether due to inadequate sales to cover expenses and/or the misappropriate of funds. The total debt will be divided equally across all company employees.

_____ (Signature)   _____ (Date)

_____ (Signature)   _____ (Date)

_____ (Signature)   _____ (Date)

_____ (Signature)   _____ (Date)

_____ (Signature)   _____ (Date)

_____ (Signature)   _____ (Date)

_____ (Signature)   _____ (Date)

> Have every team member sign and date one copy of the report.

Appendix—Survey

Product Survey

There's no obligation to purchase anything, we just need your feedback for a business class. The questions below refer to the shirt below which is being proposed for Harold's Barbeque:

1. Have you ever eaten at Harold's Barbeque?
   ___ yes
   ___ no

2. How likely would you be to buy a Harold's t-shirt ?
   ___ very likely
   ___ maybe
   ___ not likely

3. Where would you place Harold's logo on a t-shirt?
   ___ front
   ___ back

4. What's the maximum price you'd be willing to pay?
   ___ $8
   ___ $10
   ___ $13
   ___ $14
   ___ $16

5. What size t-shirt do you usually wear?
   ___ small
   ___ medium
   ___ large
   ___ XL
   ___ XXL

6. What color t-shirt do you think would look better?
   ___ red
   ___ yellow

Appendix—Better Business Bureau Endorsement

Reliability Report for

Excel Screenprinting

A BBB Accredited business since 04/21/1999.

The BBB reports on businesses, both accredited and non-accredited. If a company is a BBB Accredited business, it is stated in this report.

Name:	Levrets Office Machines
Phone:	(325) 695-1250
Fax:	(325) 698-0948
Address:	4101 Sayles Blvd
	Abilene, TX 79605-7214
Original Business Start Date:	April 1994
Principal:	Tim Levrets
Customer Contact:	Tim Levrets
Email Address:	timlevrets@levrets.com
Entity:	Corporation
Incorporated:	April 1967, TX
Employees:	7
TOB Classification:	Office Furniture & Equipment, Copiers & Copier Supplies
BBB Accreditation:	This organization is a BBB Accredited business.

> If your supplier is not listed with the BBB, omit this appendix. But be prepared to describe your due diligence.

BBB Accreditation Status

This company has been a BBB Accredited business since April 1999. This means it supports the BBB's services to the public and meets our BBB Accreditation standards.

Program Participation

This company participates in the BBB Accreditation Identification Program and has agreed to use special procedures including **arbitration**, if necessary, to resolve disputes.

Nature Of Business

Repair and sell office equipment

Customer Experience

Based on BBB files, this company has a **satisfactory record** with the BBB. A **satisfactory record** means a company has been in business for at least 12 months, and properly addressed matters referred by the BBB. The company does not have an unusual volume of complaints, or any government actions involving its marketplace conduct. The BBB understands and has no concerns about the company's products, services and type of business.

The BBB processed a total of 0 complaints about this company in the last 36 months, our standard reporting period.

Report as of November 24, 2007
Copyright© 2007 BBB®, Inc.

12

Appendix—Contract

I, Harold Jones, hereby give my permission for the Venture Out group Team Harold's to utilize the logo that I provided them on Wednesday, the 26th of September, 2008, for the production of t-shirts. I understand that they will not desecrate or misrepresent this symbol in any way. I understand that they will not do anything to the logo that would be detrimental or demeaning to Harold's or anybody else. I am aware that the making of this shirt is a one time project and will not exceed the time constraints of the date signed until the 14th of December, 2008. I am also aware that all profits from these sales will be given to Special Olympics Texas, and will not be used for the personal spending of any member of Team Harold's.

_____   _____
(Signature)   (Date)

> If you are using a name, photograph, or logo that requires a contract, include it. If you have a single customer—such as a club—include a signed contract stating that they will buy your product at an agreed upon price. (Be sure they sign off on a prototype and you keep them informed throughout the process.)

TASK 7: FUNDING & ORDERING

"Even the grandest project depends on the success of the smallest components."

~ The New Dictionary of Cultural Literacy *definition for "The devil is in the details"*

OVERVIEW

- Present your business plan to the Loan Review Board (selected team members)
- Make revisions requested by Loan Review Board (TEAM)
- Order your product and purchase budgeted materials as needed (MARP)
- Team check (TEAM)

DETAILS

1. Present your business plan to the Loan Review Board (selected team members)

   Be sure to arrive on time to your loan review appointment. Dress professionally and double-check that you have all your presentation materials. You may be meeting with members of the business community such as local bankers, consultants, and entrepreneurs. Whoever are your judges, they have given their time to consider your plan. Your instructor will tell you where and when to meet. Be sure to bring three copies of your business plan for the Loan Review Board judges and any additional copies you may wish to use.

2. Make revisions requested by Loan Review Board (if relevant) (TEAM)

   If the Loan Review Board suggests any alterations in your budget, sales projections, or other aspects of your business plan, amend your proposal as soon as possible. If the Loan Review Board does not approve your plan, your instructor will instruct you on next steps.

3. Order your product and purchase other budgeted materials (MARP)

   If your loan was approved, the sooner you order your product, the sooner you can start selling and delivering your product to customers! Your instructor will inform you of the procedures for obtaining funding and being reimbursed for expenses after you are approved by the Loan Review Board.

   In preparing your loan review, you should have obtained an estimate from your supplier specifying when your product will be delivered, its complete cost, and what the return policy is. It's a good idea to have this in front of you when you order to forestall a change in price or order details.

4. Team check (TEAM)

   If you haven't done it lately, today is a good day to pause and assess your team's effectiveness. Conclude today by honestly discussing the following questions:

   - What have we done well as a team?
   - What's keeping us as a team from functioning even better?
   - What action could we take to enhance our team performance?

   Avoid blaming or accusing other team members. If there are serious performance issues—such as some members are working hard but others are not—recall your agreed upon accountability principles and commit to an action plan that will address these problems. Communicate honestly, assertively, and tactfully. Involve your coach and/or instructor if needed. Your instructor may have a procedure for addressing a team member who has not been involved. If you want to know more, just ask.

   Sales are about to begin!

TASK 8: SELLING

"Unless you try to do something beyond what you have already mastered, you will never grow."

~ Ronald E. Osborn

OVERVIEW

- Review your sales policy, schedule, and logistics with the team (MARP)
- Advertise your product (MARP)
- Compare expenditures with the team budget (FINA)
- Report your team sales totals to your instructor (MARP)
- Sell, Sell, Sell! (TEAM)
- Manage your business processes (MARP; FINA; MGMT; TEAM)

DETAILS

1. Review your sales policy, schedule, and logistics with the team (MARP)

    Insure everyone is clear on the sales schedule and expectations for each team member. Review who will sell, how much, when, and where. Design any forms needed to track inventory, sales, and any policy or logistics regulating sales such as who brings the product to the sales point (if applicable), what records are kept, who receives sales money until it can be deposited, how often deposits will occur, what happens at the end of a sales shift if the next person doesn't show (if applicable), etc. Work with the FINA group and comply with any cash management policies they have adopted. Is a discussion of sales techniques or a sales pitch helpful?

2. Advertise your product (MARP)

    If you are advertising, now's the time to start implementing your plan. Abide by any rules or regulations in advertising on your campus (e.g., where flyers can be posted and if they must be pre-approved, email regulations, etc.).

3. Compare expenditures with the team budget (FINA)

   Although no further reminders will be given, keep an eye on expenditures, insuring they remain within budget or that you have sufficient funds to pay for any unforeseen overages. Manage the budget as financial directors and team members. Insure everyone knows of your approval process for making purchases and retain whatever documentation is needed for reimbursement.

4. Sell, Sell, Sell! (TEAM)

   Early in the selling period is the best time to maximize sales. Sell professionally, respecting those you approach. Work hard, motivate everyone to participate, be ethical.

5. Manage your business processes (MARP; FINA; MGMT; TEAM)

   - Marketing and Production (MARP): If you have adequate processes and data gathering tools in place, you'll know which team members have product checked out and how many units they have remaining. You'll know who is selling the most, how well your products are selling, and whether a change in promotion or price may be needed. Compare your actual performance with your sales projections in your business plan and work hard to stay on or ahead of your goals.

   - Finance and Accounting (FINA): It is imperative to the success of your group that you continue to keep careful controls on money handling and accounting. Precision, accountability, and security are often critical. It's important that you not keep large sums of cash where they could be lost or stolen. Collect and deposit cash often!

   - Management (MGMT): Look ahead to the annual report and be sure you are collecting items along the way, including meeting minutes and any documents you'll need. If you have one or more team member who is uninvolved at this point, problem-solve what action is appropriate. Visit with your instructor if needed.

   - Team (TEAM): If there are problems in company functioning, take a moment to discuss those openly.

The three-quarter mark is often the hardest point in a race. Keep moving forward!

TASK 9: REPORTING

"It usually takes me more than three weeks to prepare a good impromptu speech."

~ Mark Twain

OVERVIEW

- Assemble a professional annual report (MGMT with the help of all members)

DETAILS

1. Assemble a professional annual report (MGMT with the help of all team members)

   Like the business plan, the annual report will require some time to be complete and professional. It has fewer elements than your business plan (although it's about 9 to 12 pages) and asks you to reflect about your team and group performance. Groups are indicated by items they may be able to provide. Include all elements listed in the order given. As with the business plan, you can be creative in developing your own look and feel to the report. Photographs can be used throughout the report as can graphs and charts where they add value. This is the culmination of your Venture Out experience and the last time to work together as a team—stay motivated and help each other produce a superior report!

ANNUAL REPORT CHECKLIST

Cover Page {1 page}

- ❏ Company name (MGMT)
- ❏ Team photo (MGMT)
- ❏ Company mission statement (MGMT)

Letter to Shareholders {1 page}

- ❏ A letter from the CEO is often the first item in an annual report. (You can find examples on corporate Web sites; just look under the "Investors" or "Shareholder Relations" tab.) Summarize your Venture Out team's overall performance in a brief letter. Did you accomplish your goals? Did you function well as a team? Did you provide the service and financial return that your customers and investors might expect? If you were continuing as a company, would you be positioned as a strong and growing competitor? In areas where you're weaker, what plans would you put in place to address any significant problems? (Tip: You might have to imagine a bit here but give it a try.) (MGMT)

Group Reflections {3 to 6 pages}

Each group (FINA; MARP; MGMT) should prepare a 1- to 2-page report which includes the following elements:

- ❏ Group Photo
- ❏ Reflections – Think back about your actions and effectiveness as a group, from the start of Venture Out to the end. What did you do well? What challenges did you face? How did you address problems? How well did you follow your company rules and boundaries which you established in Task 2? Why or why not? What might you have done even better? (Take the lessons learned to your next student or work group.)
- ❏ What recommendations would you offer to future Venture Out teams and groups?

Marketing Performance {1 page}

- ❏ Include a table or chart showing the number of products sold by each team member (MARP)

Financial Performance {1 page} – examples are provided at the end of this checklist

- ❏ Balance Sheet (FINA)
- ❏ Income Statement (FINA)
- ❏ Statement of Cash Flows (FINA)

Appendices {about 2 pages}

- ❏ Minutes of group meetings (MGMT)
- ❏ Directory of employee names, phone numbers, and e-mail addresses (MGMT)
- ❏ Name and address of beneficiary (if applicable) (MARP)

FINANCIAL STATEMENT EXAMPLES

Your financial statements will follow the format that accountants use, but they'll be simple. Even if you've not had an accounting class, you'll be able to prepare these. Yours may differ slightly if you have some special categories of expenditures or revenue, unsold or damaged goods, or other unique occurrences. If you have a question, just ask your instructor.

	Team Harold's **Balance Sheet**	
		2008
Assets		
Cash		$289.76
Total Assets		$289.76
Liabilities and Owners' Equity		
Total Liabilities		$0.00
Retained Earnings		$289.76
Total Liabilities and Owners' Equity		$289.76

	Team Harold's **Income Statement** For the Period Ending Dec. 31, 2008	
Revenues (Gross Sales)		$910.00
Cost of Goods Sold:		
Shirts	$603.50	
Total		$603.50
Gross Profit		$306.50
Operating Expenses:		
Posterboard	$0.41	
Shipping	$6.17	
Folders	$7.10	
Cash Box	$3.06	
Total		$16.74
Net Income		$289.76

[Handwritten note next to Operating Expenses: "Sales tax Paid"]

Team Harold's
Statement of Cash Flows
For Period Ending December 31, 2008

Cash, Beginning of Year	$0.00
Net Income	$289.76
Cash, End of Year	$289.76

TASK 10: CELEBRATING

"Courage is only an accumulation of small steps"

~ George Konrad

OVERVIEW

- Complete a peer evaluation (TEAM)
- Celebrate! (TEAM)

DETAILS

1. Complete a peer evaluation (TEAM)

    If you haven't done so already, your instructor may request that you evaluate yourself and/or each of your team members. If asked to do so, please complete the evaluation honestly and confidentially and turn it in on time.

    If you've been communicating throughout the semester, no one should be surprised by the evaluation they receive. Now's not the time for vindictiveness, but by the same token, you owe your peers an honest, *formative* evaluation—one that is neither inflated nor condemnatory. Rather than artificially praising or being acerbic, reflect on team members' strengths and help them to become stronger.

2. Celebrate! (TEAM)

    You made it! Take the lessons learned in Venture Out with you to your next entrepreneurial and team experience.

APPENDIX: FREQUENTLY ASKED QUESTIONS

PRODUCTS

Can we sell services?

Unless allowed by your instructor, services—like putting on a benefit concert or providing car detailing—generally are discouraged. There are two reasons for this. One is that services provide less opportunity to learn about inventory management, budgeting, and debt financing—important skills in many businesses. Second, no one shows up, you don't have anything of value to sell, thus the risk could be quite high. A product can be reviewed by the Loan Review Board which at least provides an external review of a tangible asset.

Can we sell a group of products?

Generally, it's best to focus on a single product. One product allows you to more clearly focus on and understand market demand, pricing, and sales. In investments, business, and entire economies, diversification often reduces risk. But in start-ups, diversification may cause you to lose focus on your market. Sometimes teams want to sell two products because they can't resolve differences of opinion among team members. If that's the case, keep working with the team's process and ask your instructor to help if necessary.

Does the supplier have to be local?

Based on the experience of past Venture Out companies, a local supplier can save you a lot of grief. Although you may have to pay state sales tax and perhaps slightly more for the product, local suppliers are often speedy. If there's a problem, you can talk with them face-to-face. You can sometimes inspect samples before you order and don't have to drive long distances or be surprised when something besides what you thought you were ordering, arrives in the mail. You'll contribute to the local economy too if you order local.

If you order from an Internet vendor, proceed with care and get all your specifics in writing. Images can look larger or a different color on a computer screen than in person, so attend carefully to product descriptions. Not all suppliers—local or non-local—are reputable. Not all are easy to work with when problems emerge. For any supplier, do due diligence—get prices, delivery guarantees, and return policies in writing, and check references.

Can we use a school logo on our product?

Your instructor will provide important instruction about the use of school logos, mascots, names, or trademarked images. Universities protect their brands and often have detailed regulations covering their use. Learning about graphic design and copyright, trademark, and patent law is part of Venture Out.

May we use original artwork or phrases or artwork from the Internet?

Even if you create a design or phrase, be sure to clear it with your instructor early in the product design process. You may have a team member who is an accomplished artist, or perhaps you have a friend outside of class who is good at graphic design. Before they devote a lot of time to crafting an image or design for reproduction on your company product, it's wise to follow steps often used in industry:

- Be sure you know the type of image you need—the size, color, amount of detail, and format required by the supplier. Embroidery, for example, may not allow fine details. Reversing an image's colors may make it unclear, and so forth. Think about the constraints of the format before you commission art work.

- Work up a rough sketch of the idea and show it to your instructor to approve. If the design refers to your institution, you may also need to get an okay from the office on your campus that handles all school marketing. Some schools do not allow alternate renditions of mascots or logos.

- Only after you do the first two steps should you have a final art work completed.

How edgy can a product be?

As in business, you'll want to weigh legal, ethical, and responsible aspects of your actions. Some state laws allow limited parodies of people or trademarked phrases or copyrighted images. But there are limits. Carefully consider issues of ethics, social responsibility, and how your product might impact your instructor, peers, school, and community. If the Loan Review Board judges think your product is questionable, they may send you back to the drawing board.

SALES

Where can we sell?

Special permission is needed from your instructor if you wish to sell off-campus or to individuals other than students. Additionally, your campus probably has regulations governing what types of products can be sold, who can sell products, where advertisements can be placed, and so forth. Anticipate making most of your sales to other students. A portion of your sales may be allowed to parents, friends, or others. Avoid unwelcome solicitations or pressuring people. Spam e-mails are not allowed.

FINANCE

How does the loan review work?

After choosing a product, your team will prepare a business plan to present to a group of entrepreneurs, bankers, and/or other professionals. Your instructor may attend the presentation, as may upper-level business students interested in entrepreneurship.

If our loan is approved, how will we be given our money?

Your instructor may distribute your loan to you in cash, or may extend a "line of credit," paying for your product expense and reimbursing you for approved expenses up to the total of your loan amount. Be sure to keep a copy of your invoices since they will be required for reimbursement. Your instructor will tell you more before or at the time of the loan review.

What is the largest loan we can request?

Your institution will set a maximum you can request. Remember, the more you borrow, the more sales are required to pay it back. A wise entrepreneur goes for the minimum financing which will cover expenses. Calculate your needs carefully and operate lean.

Are we charged interest on our loan?

Check your institution specific instructions or ask your instructor.

Do we charge sales tax?

Check your institution specific instructions or ask your instructor.

Are our purchases or the purchases made by our customers tax deductible?

Check your institution specific instructions or ask your instructor.

Do we accept checks?

Check your institution specific instructions or ask your instructor.

What happens if we don't make a profit?

While a lot can be learned in failing, Venture Out will succeed if you make wise decisions at each step. You'll feel the pressure to be profitable, just like start-ups do. If you don't break even, the team is still responsible for repaying the loan—fiscal responsibility is required, just like in business. There is no bankruptcy provision.

Who gets the profits?

Businesses exchange resources—materials and people—for goods and services. Thus, they have a responsibility to benefit the communities and investors. Rather than benefiting yourself, you'll likely share your profits with others. Check your institution specific information. If you are giving profits to a beneficiary, you may want to let your customers know as an added benefit of their purchase.

TEAM

What do you do when a minority of team members is doing all the work?

This often occurs when some individuals care about their evaluation and they don't want to risk their grade to others' effort, or lack of effort. Those who care somewhat less about grades may assume they will earn acceptable marks by allowing overachievers to do the work. Occasionally, this imbalance in work load occurs when someone finds it more efficient to do the work themselves rather than allow less experienced members to bumble along. In yet other cases, a team member may be distracted by life or work events or obligations outside of class. For whatever reason, less learning occurs when team members are not equally and fully engaged. You'll have to decide how legitimate the reason is for workload imbalances, but if you keep your eye on learning rather than the easy way out, you'll earn more dividends from Venture Out.

What if we find ourselves behind on report writing, ordering, and/or sales?

Time pressure can motivate, but if you allow too little time for a task you may overlook a creative solution or miss a fatal flaw. Solving this may be as simple as setting team deadlines which allow some buffer before the class deadline. Set a deadline a few days before, break up tasks into small units, follow-up with assignments taken, and manage your team process so everyone works hard to meet the deadline.

What if a product is selected with poor market information or market research is ignored?

You increase your risk of lagging sales if you haven't asked the right sample the right questions. Sometimes, however, a team has consulted the market and goes against their advice on product design or pricing. You may be able to make up the lackluster reception in your sales pitch, or you may suspect the data is unrepresentative of your population, but have a good reason and a strategy if you cut against the grain of your customers.

How do we address team problems?

Ignoring team conflict can be effective at times. Choosing your battles, being flexible, compromise—these allow room for unique opinions and personalities. Often, however, ignoring problems becomes dysfunctional itself. Everyone knows something is not working but no one is doing anything about it. See this as an opportunity for your team to pull closer together and develop team skills that you can take with you after Venture Out. Immensely practical guidance on communication is available from books produced by the Harvard Negotiation Project.[5] As always, you can invite counsel from your instructor too.

Can we fire a team member?

If you've exhausted all alternatives, your instructor may allow you to fire a team member. Teamwork is often challenging. When done well, it is rewarding, and even more so when you work through a challenge together. At first, conflicts may be suppressed, but eventually, it often occurs in group work.

If you have a team member who is not contributing, talk with them. The person may not know they are underperforming or causing team problems. They may not understand the team's expectations. Hear them out and allow for feelings to be expressed but keep your focus on team performance rather than on blaming or sorting through who said or did what. Consider whether it's an ability, motivation, communication, perception, or personality problem. If it's an ability problem or personality clash, consider shifting the team member to a new task or group. If it's a motivation problem, communicate the consequences of underperformance for the company and student. If it's communication, clarify team expectations.

If a member is completely uninvolved, the team may take steps toward more serious corrective action. Your instructor may have a time limit on how late this can occur during Venture Out. Consult him or her on how to proceed.

ASSESSMENT

How are we graded?

See your syllabus or instructions from your instructor.

OTHER

Don't hesitate to ask your instructor. He/She wants you to be successful. Be proactive in seeking out answers and involving good counsel.

---

[5] Regarding communication, consult Douglas Stone, Bruce Patton, and Sheila Heen's excellent work, *Difficult Conversations* (New York: Penguin, 1999). For negotiating with team members, try Roger Fisher and William Ury's classic, *Getting to Yes* (New York: Penguin, 1981).